Bedtime Prayers
FOR THE FAMILY

ENDING THE DAY TOGETHER WITH PRAYER

W PUBLISHING GROUP
A Division of Thomas Nelson Publishers
Since 1798

www.wpublishinggroup.com

Bedtime Prayers for the Family
Copyright © 2005 W Publishing Group.

W Publishing books may be purchased in bulk for educational, business, fund-raising, or sales promotional use. For information, please e-mail SpecialMarkets@ThomasNelson.com.

Published by W Publishing Group, a division of Thomas Nelson, Inc., P.O. Box 141000, Nashville, Tennessee 37214.

Unless otherwise indicated, Scripture quotations used in this book are from THE NEW KING JAMES VERSION (NKJV). Copyright © 1979, 1980, 1982 by Thomas Nelson, Inc. All rights reserved.

Scripture quotations noted NIV are from the HOLY BIBLE, NEW INTERNATIONAL VERSION®. Copyright © 1973, 1978, 1984 by International Bible Society. Used by permission of Zondervan Publishing House. All rights reserved.

Scripture quotations noted KJV are from the KING JAMES VERSION of the Holy Bible.

Selections for this edition of Bedtime Prayers for the Family were made by Elizabeth Kea.

Library of Congress Cataloging-in-Publication Data

Bed time prayers for the family : ending the day together with prayer.
    p. cm.
    ISBN 0-8499-1846-4
    1. Family—Prayer-books and devotions—English. 2. Prayers. 3. Family—Religious life. I. W Publishing Group.
    BV255.B38 2005
    242'.8—dc22

                                                        2004029436

Printed in the United States of America

05 06 07 08 QWM 6 5 4 3 2 1

CONTENTS

INTRODUCTION

If your family is like most, bedtime may be the only time of day when everyone's activities have slowed down and you are able to spend a few moments together. You may chat about the successes and failures of the day, or plans for the following day, then, before turning out the lights, thank the One who created the day and who now gently draws it to a close. Perhaps your bedtime prayers are ones you learned when you were small and now recite to your own children, or perhaps you and your family simply pray whatever is on your heart each evening. Whatever way you speak with God at bedtime, we hope that *Bedtime Prayers for the Family* will be a source of inspiration and comfort as your family shares this important time.

We have included prayers from believers who come from many different walks of life, but all share a desire to thank God for His goodness, to know Him more intimately, and to be always under His watchful care. May their prayers capture the very heart of your desires as well and give words to your petitions.

This book is divided into six sections. We offer "Reflections on the Day" as a means to look back on your day and see God's involvement—in both the gracious blessings and the confusing trials. "Prayers of Comfort and Peace" will be like a warm blanket, enveloping you in the love and peace of your Father who holds all things in His care and control. "As I Lay Me Down to Sleep" contains bedtime prayers that ask God for His protection and balm of rest throughout the night. "Bedtime Prayers for Others" reminds us of those who most need our prayers at night—the lonely, the sick, and those pouring out their lives for God's service. "Bedtime Prayers for Holidays and Memorable Days" includes prayers with which to close joyful, celebratory days, such as birthdays, Christmas, and Easter, as well as prayers for memorable yet sad days, such as after the death of a loved one or when moving.

We have also compiled a large selection of children's prayers that you can read to your children when they are young, or they can read themselves as they grow older. This section includes many familiar classics, as well as lighthearted prayers that are sure to become your children's favorites.

We hope *Bedtime Prayers for the Family* will be a treasury your family will enjoy for many years to come. May it inspire you to close your days by thanking God for His goodness and by asking Him to draw you closer and closer to His heart.

—Elizabeth Kea

I.

Reflections on the Day

HIS SURPRISES

The day is drenched in Thee:
In little, exquisite surprises
Bubbling deliciousness of Thee arises
From sudden places,
Under the common traces
Of my most lethargied and 'custom paces.

—AMY CARMICHAEL

PIED BEAUTY

Glory be to God for dappled things—
For skies of couple-colour as a brinded cow;
For rose-moles all in stipple upon trout that swim;
Fresh-firecoal chestnut falls; finches' wings;
Landscape plotted and pieced—fold, fallow, and
   plough;
And all trades, their gear and tackle and trim.
All things counter, original, spare, strange;
Whatever is fickle, freckled (who knows how?)
With swift, slow; sweet, sour; adazzle, dim;
He fathers-forth whose beauty is past change:
Praise him.

—GERALD MANLEY HOPKINS

A GRATEFUL HEART

Thou hast given so much to me,
Give one thing more—a grateful heart;
Not thankful when it pleaseth me,
As if Thy blessings had spare days;
But such a heart, whose pulse may be
Thy praise.

—GEORGE HERBERT

Prayers

ON EACH RETURN OF NIGHT

*O*n each return of night, consider how the past day has been spent by us, what have been our prevailing thoughts, words, and actions during it, and how far we can acquit ourselves of evil. Have we thought irreverently of Thee, have we disobeyed Thy commandments, have we neglected any known duty, or willingly given pain to any human being? Incline us to ask our hearts these questions, O God, and save us from deceiving ourselves by pride or vanity.

Give us a thankful sense of the blessings in which we live, of the many comforts of our lot; that we may not deserve to lose them by discontent or indifference.

Be gracious to our necessities, and guard us, and all we love, from evil this night. May the sick and afflicted be now and ever Thy care, and heartily do we pray for the safety of all that travel by land or by sea, for the comfort and protection of the orphan and widow, and that Thy pity may be shown upon all captives and prisoners.

Above all other blessings, O God, for ourselves, and our fellow-creatures, we implore Thee to quicken our sense of Thy mercy in the redemption of the world, of the value of that holy religion in which we have been brought up, that we may not, by our own neglect, throw away the salvation Thou hast given us, nor be Christians only in name. Hear us, Almighty God, for His sake who has redeemed us, and taught us thus to pray.

—JANE AUSTEN

GRACE BEFORE SLEEP

How can our minds and bodies be
Grateful enough that we have spent
Here in this generous room, we three,
This evening of content?
Each one of us has walked through storm
And fled the wolves along the road;
But here the hearth is wide and warm,
And for this shelter and this light
Accept, O Lord, our thanks tonight.

—SARA TEASDALE

THE DAY THOU GAVEST, LORD, IS ENDED

The day Thou gavest, Lord, is ended,
The darkness falls at Thy behest;
To Thee our morning hymns ascended,
Thy praise shall sanctify our rest.
We thank Thee that Thy Church, unsleeping,
While earth rolls onward into light,
Through all the world her watch is keeping,
And rests not now by day or night.
As o'er each continent and island
The dawn leads on another day,
The voice of prayer is never silent,
Nor dies the strain of praise away.
The sun that bids us rest is waking
Our brethren 'neath the western sky,
And hour by hour fresh lips are making
Thy wondrous doings heard on high.
So be it, Lord; Thy throne shall never,
Like earth's proud empires, pass away:
Thy kingdom stands, and grows forever,
Till all Thy creatures own Thy sway.

—JOHN ELLERTON

EVENING PRAISE

*G*iver of All,
Another day is ended
and I take my place beneath my
great Redeemer's cross,
where healing streams continually descend,
where balm is poured into every wound,
where I wash anew in the all-cleansing blood,
assured that thou seest in me no spots of sin.
Yet a little while and I shall go to thy
home and be no more seen;
help me to gird up the loins of my mind,
to quicken my step,
to speed as if moment were my last,
that my life be joy, my death glory.
I thank thee for the temporal blessings of this world—
the refreshing air,
the light of the sun,
the food that renews strength,

the raiment that clothes,

the dwelling that shelters,

the sleep that gives rest,

the starry canopy of night,

the summer breeze,

the flowers' sweetness,

the music of flowing streams,

the happy endearments of family, kindred, friends.

Things animate, things inanimate, minister to my

comfort.

My cup runs over.

Suffer me not to be insensible to these daily mercies.

Thy hand bestows blessings: thy power averts evil.

I bring my tribute of thanks for spiritual graces,

the full warmth of faith,

the cheering presence of thy Spirit,

the strength of thy restraining will,

thy spiking of hell's artillery.

Blessed be my sovereign Lord!

—THE VALLEY OF VISION

GIVING THANKS

It is good to give thanks to the LORD,
And to sing praises to Your name, O Most High;
To declare Your lovingkindness in the morning,
And Your faithfulness every night . . .
For You, LORD, have made me glad through Your work;
I will triumph in the works of Your hands.

—PSALM 92:1, 2, 4

DAILY BLESSINGS

For the love that like a screen
Sheltered from the might-have-been;
For that fire could never burn us,
Deeps could never drown or turn us;
For our daily blessings, Lord,
Be Thy name adored.

For the gentle joys that pass
Like the dew upon the grass,
New each morning, lighting duty
With a radiance and a beauty;
For our daily blessings, Lord,
Be Thy name adored.

Many a storm has threatened loud,
And then melted like a cloud,
Seeking to distress, confound us,
Met Thy great wings folded round us;
For our daily blessings, Lord,
Be Thy name adored.

—AMY CARMICHAEL

I LOVE TO STEAL AWHILE AWAY

I love to steal awhile away

From every cumbering care,

And spend the hours of closing day

In humble, grateful, prayer.

I love to think on mercies past,

And future good implore,

And all my cares and sorrows cast

On God, whom I adore.

I love by faith to take a view

Of brighter scenes in heaven;

The prospect doth my strength renew,

While here by tempests driven.

Thus, when life's toilsome day is o'er,

May its departing ray,

Be calm at this impressive hour,

And lead to endless day.

—PHOEBE H. BROWN

FEELING DEFEATED

*L*ord, I have been so defeated by circumstances. I have felt like an animal trapped in a corner with nowhere to flee. Where are you in all this, Lord? The night is dark. I cannot feel Your presence.

Help me to know that the darkness is really "shade of Your hand, outstretched caressingly"; that the "hemming in" is Your doing. Perhaps there was no other way You could get my full attention, no other way I would allow You to demonstrate what You can do in my life.

I see now that the emptier my cup is, the more space there is to receive Your love and supply.

—CATHERINE MARSHALL

AFTER A LONG DAY

God of our life,
There are days when the burdens we carry
Chafe our shoulders and weigh us down;
When the road seems dreary and endless,
The skies gray and threatening;
When our lives have no music in them,
And our hearts are lonely,
And our souls have lost their courage.
Flood the path with light,
Run our eyes to where
The skies are full of promise;
Tune our hearts to brave music;
Give us the sense of comradeship
With heroes and saints of every age;
And so quicken our spirits
That we may be able to encourage
The souls of all who journey with us
On the road of life, to your honor and glory.

—SAINT AUGUSTINE

TOO MANY WORDS

*O*Lord, I have been talking to the people;
Thought's wheels have round me whirled a fiery zone,
And the recoil of my words' airy ripple
My heart unheedful has puffed up and blown.
Therefore I cast myself before thee prone:
Lay cool hands on my burning brain, and press
From my weak heart the swelling emptiness.

—GEORGE MACDONALD

MY DAY IS ENDING

*L*ord,
You have been with me all through this day,
stay with me now.
As the shadows lengthen into darkness
let the noisy world grow quiet,
let its feverish concerns be stilled,
its voices silenced.
In the final moments of this day
remind me of what is real.

But let me not forget
that you were as present in
the stresses of the day just past
as you are now
in the silence of this night.

You have made me for
day and for night,
for work and for rest,
for both heaven and earth.

Here in this night
let me embrace and not regret
the mysterious beauty of my humanity.
Keep me in the embrace of your reality
through the night,
and the day to come.
Surround me with your silence
and give me the rest that only you can give—
real peace,
now and forever.

—JOHN KIRVAN

EVENING

O Holiest Truth! How have I lied to Thee!
I vow'd this day Thy festival should be:
But I aim dim ere the night.
Surely I made my prayer and did deem
That I could keep in me the morning beam,
Immaculate and bright;
But my foot slipp'd; and as I lay, he came,
My gloomy foe, and robb'd me of heaven's flame.
Help Thou my darkness, Lord, till I ma light.

—JOHN HENRY NEWMAN

DEAR LORD, FORGIVE

If I have wounded any soul today,
If I have caused one foot to go astray,
If I have walked in my own willful way,
Dear Lord, forgive!

If I have uttered idle words or vain,
If I have turned aside from want or pain,
Lest I myself shall suffer through the strain,
Dear Lord, forgive!

If I have been perverse or hard, or cold,
If I have longed for shelter in Thy fold,
When Thou hast given me some fort to hold,
Dear Lord, forgive!

Forgive the sins I have confessed to Thee;
Forgive the secret sins I do not see;
O guide me, love me, and my keeper be,
Dear Lord, Amen.

—C. Maude Battersby

SUNSET

For the great red rose of sunset,
Dropping petals on the way
For the tired feet of day—
Thanks to Thee, our Father.

For the violet of twilight
Singing, "Hush, ye children, hush";
For the afterglow's fair flush—
Thanks to Thee, our Father.

For the softly sliding darkness
Wherein many jewels are
Kindly-eyed familiar—
Thanks to Thee, our Father.

For the comfort of forgiveness
Taking from us our offence,
Steeping us in innocence—
Thanks to Thee, our Father.

For the viewless, tall white angels
Bidden to ward off from us
All things foul, calamitous—
Thanks to Thee, our Father.

That Thy love sets not with sunset,
Nor with starset, nor with moon,
But is ever one high noon—
Thanks to Thee, our Father.

—AMY CARMICHAEL

Prayers

AND NOW THIS HOLY DAY

And now this holy day
Is drawing to its end,
Once more, to Thee, O Lord,
Our thanks and prayers we send.
We thank Thee for this rest
From earthly care and strife;
We thank Thee for this help
To higher, holier life.
Yet, ere we go to rest,
Father, to Thee we pray,
Forgive the sins that stain
E'en this Thy holy day.
Through Jesus let the past
Be blotted from Thy sight,
And let us all now sleep
At peace with Thee this night.
To God the Father, Son,
And Spirit glory be,
From all in earth and Heav'n,
Through all eternity.

—EDWARD HARLAND

As Now the Sun's Declining Rays

As now the sun's declining rays
At eventide descend,
So life's brief day is sinking down
To its appointed end.
Lord, on the cross Thine arms were stretched,
To draw Thy people nigh;
O grant us then that cross to love,
And in those arms to die.
All glory to the Father be,
All glory to the Son,
All glory, Holy Ghost, to Thee,
While endless ages run.

—CHARLES COFFIN

An Evening Prayer

Lord, Jesus Christ, under your loving
gaze I consider the activities of my day.
Thank you for:
the warmth of the sun,
the affirmation of friends,
the help of fellow workers.
Forgive me for:
looking to my own interests,
failing to encourage others,
neglecting the weak.
By faith I now enter the darkness of the night,
declaring, "It is well with my soul."
Amen.

—Richard Foster

AN EVENING PRAYER

I give Thee praise, O God, for a well-spent day. But I am yet unsatisfied, because I do not enjoy enough of Thee. I would have my soul more closely united to Thee by faith and love. I would love Thee above all things. Thou, who hast made me, knowest my desires, my expectations. My joys all center in Thee and it is Thou Thyself that I desire; it is Thy favour, Thine acceptance, the communications of Thy grace that I earnest wish for, more than anything in the world. I rejoice in Thine essential glory and blessedness. I rejoice in my relation to Thee, who art my Father, my Lord, and my God. I rejoice that Thou hast power over me and that I desire to live in subjection to Thee. I thank Thee that Thou hast brought me so far. I will beware of despairing of Thy mercy for the time that is to come, and will give Thee the glory of Thy free grace. Amen.

—SUSANNA WESLEY

DAY IS DYING IN THE WEST

Day is dying in the west;
Heav'n is touching earth with rest;
Wait and worship while the night
Sets the evening lamps alight
Through all the sky.

Holy, holy, holy, Lord God of Hosts!
Heav'n and earth are full of Thee!
Heav'n and earth are praising Thee,
O Lord most high!

Lord of life, beneath the dome
Of the universe, Thy home,
Gather us who seek Thy face
To the fold of Thy embrace,
For Thou art nigh.

While the deepening shadows fall,
Heart of love enfolding all,
Through the glory and the grace
Of the stars that veil Thy face,
Our hearts ascend.

When forever from our sight
Pass the stars, the day, the night,
Lord of angels, on our eyes
Let eternal morning rise
And shadows end.

—MARY LATHBURY

DISPOSE OUR HEARTS

Father of Heaven, whose goodness has brought us in safety to the close of this day, dispose our hearts in fervent prayer. Another day is now gone, and added to those for which we were before accountable. Teach us, Almighty Father, to consider this solemn truth, as we should do, that we may feel the importance of every day, and every hour as it passes, and earnestly strive to make a better use of what Thy goodness may yet bestow on us, than we have done this time past.

—JANE AUSTEN

FOR SUCCESS

*L*ord, behold our family here assembled. We thank Thee for this place in which we dwell; for the love that unites us; for the peace accorded us this day; for the hope with which we expect the morrow; for the health, the work, the food, and the bright skies that make our lives delightful; for our friends in all parts of the earth.

Let peace abound in our small company. Purge out of every heart the lurking grudge. Give us grace and strength to forbear and persevere. Give us the grace to accept and forgive offenders.

Forgetful ourselves, help us to bear cheerfully the forgetfulness of others. Give us courage and gaiety and the quiet mind. Spare to us our friends, soften to us our enemies. Bless us, if it may be, in all our innocent endeavors. If it may not, give us the strength to encounter that which is to come, that we be brave in peril, constant in tribulation, temperate in wrath, and in all changes of fortune, and down to the gates of death, loyal and loving one to another.

As the clay to the potter, as the windmill to the wind, as children of their sire, we beseech of Thee this help and mercy for Christ's sake.

—ROBERT LOUIS STEVENSON

THY GENTLENESS HATH MADE ME GREAT

David ascribes all his own greatness to the condescending goodness of his Father in heaven. May this sentiment be echoed in our hearts this evening while we cast our crowns at Jesus' feet and cry, "thy gentleness hath made me great." How marvelous has been our experience of God's gentleness! How gentle have been his corrections! How gentle his forbearance! How gentle his teachings! How gentle his drawings! Meditate upon this theme, O believer. Let gratitude be awakened; let humility be deepened; let love be quickened ere thou fallest asleep tonight.

—C. H. SPURGEON

II.

Prayers of Comfort and Peace

THE DAY IS DONE

The day is done, and the darkness
Falls from the wings of Night,
As a feather is wafted downward
From an eagle in his flight.

I see the lights of the village
Gleam through the rain and the mist,
And a feeling of sadness comes o'er me
That my soul cannot resist:

A feeling of sadness and longing,
That is not akin to pain,
And resembles sorrow only
As the mist resembles the rain.

Come, read to me some poem,
Some simple and heartfelt lay,

That shall soothe this restless feeling,
And banish the thoughts of day.

Not from the grand old masters,
Not from the bards sublime,
Whose distant footsteps echo
Through the corridors of Time.

For, like strains of martial music,
Their mighty thoughts suggest
Life's endless toil and endeavor;
And to-night I long for rest.

Read from some humbler poet,
Whose songs gushed from his heart,
As showers from the clouds of summer,
Or tears from the eyelids start;

Who, through long days of labor,
And nights devoid of ease,
Still heard in his soul the music
Of wonderful melodies.

Such songs have power to quiet
The restless pulse of care,
And come like the benediction
That follows after prayer.

Then read from the treasured volume
The poem of thy choice,
And lend to the rhyme of the poet
The beauty of thy voice.

And the night shall be filled with music
And the cares that infest the day,
Shall fold their tents, like the Arabs,
And as silently steal away.

—HENRY WADSWORTH LONGFELLOW

VESPERS

Twilight falls on the hill.
The west is a crumble of sundown.
From hollow and cavern and cranny
The shadows lengthen and creep.
And a slow singing of far bells
Blows on the breath of the evening
From the dim-piled crepuscular mountains
And intricate valleys of sleep.

Lamp after lamp shines forth
From the scattered farm windows below me.
A lantern moves by the rick.
Cattle low at the bars.
Comes the dull rumble of barn doors.
Voices of weary children
Dwindle into the dusk . . .
Night—and the stars!

God, if thou grantest me Heaven,

Take not this beauty from me,

But down from the lonely sky

Send thou my spirit again,

Back to the old worn ways

Of this little flickering planet—

Back to the grief and the toil

And the hopes and the homes of men.

—ODELL SHEPARD

REST

*O*n eager, hungry, busy-seeing child,
Rise up, turn round, run in, run up the stair.
Far in a chamber from rude noise exiled,
Thy Father sits, pondering how thou dost fare.
The Mighty Man will clasp thee to his breast:
Will kiss thee, stroke the tangles of thy hair,
And lap thee warm in fold on fold of lovely rest.

—GEORGE MACDONALD

I WILL BLESS THE LORD

I will bless the LORD who has given me counsel;
My heart also instructs me in the night seasons.
I have set the LORD always before me;
Because He is at my right hand I shall not be moved.
Therefore my heart is glad, and my glory rejoices;
My flesh also will rest in hope . . .
You will show me the path of life;
In Your presence is fullness of joy;
At Your right hand are pleasures forevermore.

—PSALM 16:7–9, 11

STARS

A strange surprising gladness stirs my heart
At night when heaven's first lights, dim and far,
Swing in the dusk and each one suddenly
Becomes the silver wonder of a star,

Becomes a shining splendor on the hills,
Unfailing, steadfast, calm and high and white.
Stars are so beautiful, so steeped in peace,
They rest me more than anything at night.

There is an ancient comfort in the stars—
I treasure it: "Lift up your eyes and see,"
"He calleth them by name—not one hath failed—"
Oh, often through His stars God comforts me.

—GRACE NOLL CROWELL

GAELIC PRAYER

As the rain hides the stars,
As the autumn mist hides the hills,
As the dark clouds veil the blue sky,
So the dark happenings of my lot
Hide the shining of your face from me.
Yet, if I may hold on your hand in the darkness,
It is enough.
Since I know that, though I may stumble in my going,
You do not fall.

—TRADITIONAL

MY SOUL IS CAST DOWN

O my God, my soul is cast down within me;
Therefore I will remember You from the
land of the Jordan,
And from the heights of Hermon,
From the Hill Mizar.
Deep calls unto deep at the noise of Your waterfalls;
All Your waves and billows have gone over me.
The LORD will command His
lovingkindness in the daytime,
And in the night His song shall be with me—
A prayer to the God of my life.

—PSALM 42:6–8

MOONLIGHT

*M*oonlight's tranquility:
A shimm'ring ocean, like a silver band
Between the misty sky and misty land,
And dreaming mountains sweeping to the sea.

The forest slowly heaves
And murmurs as the low night wind awakes;
The moon rides through her filmy vapors, takes
Handfuls of moonbeams, strews them on its leaves.

The shining grasses light
The fells with flow'ry arrows silver-tipped,
And their long spears are bright as though they dipped
In the dews of silver through the silver night.

Lord, when we take our part
Tomorrow in life's duty, feel the rush
Of hurrying hours, let not their passing brush
The sense of moonlit quiet from our hearts.

—AMY CARMICHAEL

An Hour with Thee

My heart is tired, so tired tonight;
How endless seems the strife—
Day after day the restlessness
Of all this weary life!
I come to lay the burden down
That so oppresseth me,
And shutting all the world without
To spend an hour with Thee,
Dear Lord,
To spend an hour with Thee.

I would forget a little while
The bitterness of tears,
The anxious thought that crowds my life
That buried hope in years;
Fraught with woman's weary toil
My patient care must be.
A tired child I come tonight
To spend an hour with Thee,
Dear Lord,
One little hour with Thee.

A foolish, wayward child, I know,
So often wandering;
A weak, complaining child—but, Oh!
Forgive my murmuring,
And fold me to Thy loving breast—
Thou who hast died for me,
And let me feel 'tis peace to rest
A little hour with Thee,
Dear Lord,
One little hour with Thee.

The bust world goes on and on,
I cannot heed it now,
Thy sacred hand is laid upon
My aching, throbbing brow.
Life's toil will soon be past, and then,
From all its sorrow free
How sweet to think that I shall spend
Eternity with Thee.
Dear Lord,
Eternity with Thee!

—MARY WHEATON LYON

IF AT NIGHT WHEN DAY IS DONE

If at night when day is done
Kneeling by your bed,
You can only think of him
Though no words are said;
If in crowds you think of him
Who gives you light and air,
God will know in his love,
That you mean a prayer.

—AUTHOR UNKNOWN

COMMUNION

Lord, I have knelt and tried to pray tonight,
But thy love came upon me like a sleep,
And all desire died out; upon the deep
Of thy mere love I lay, each thought in light
Dissolving like the sunset clouds, at rest
Each tremulous wish, and my strength weakness, sweet
As a sick boy with soon o'erwearied feet
Finds, yielding him unto his mother's breast
To weep for weakness there. I could not pray,
But with closed eyes I felt thy bosom's love
Beating toward mine, and then I would not move
Till of itself the joy should pass away;
At last my heart found voice—"Take me, O Lord,
And do with me according to thy word."

—EDWARD DOWDEN

THE DOVE

*B*lessed be the Lord for another day of mercy, even though I am now weary with its toils. Unto the preserver of men lift I my song of gratitude. The dove found no rest out of the ark, and therefore returned to it; and my soul has learned yet more fully than ever, this day, that there is no satisfaction to be found in earthly things—God alone can give rest to my spirit. As to my business, my possessions, my family, my attainments, these are all well enough in their way, but they cannot fulfill the desires of my immortal nature. Return unto thy rest, O my soul, for the Lord hath dealt bountifully with thee. It was at the still hour, when the gates of the day were closing, that with weary wing the dove came back to the master: O Lord, enable me this evening thus to return to Jesus. She could not endure to spend a night hovering over the restless waste, nor can I bear to be even for another hour away from Jesus, the rest of my heart, the home of my spirit. She did not merely alight upon the roof of the ark, she "came in to him"; even so would my longing spirit look into the secret of the Lord, pierce to the interior of truth, enter into that which is within the veil, and reach to my Beloved in very deed. To Jesus must I come: short of the nearest and dearest intercourse with him my panting spirit cannot stay. Blessed Lord Jesus, be with me, reveal thyself, and abide with me all night, so that when I awake I may be still with thee. I note that the dove brought in her mouth an olive branch plucked off, the memorial of the past day, and a prophecy of the future. Have I no leasing record to bring home? No pledge and earnest of lovingkindness yet to come? Yes, my Lord, I present thee my grateful acknowledgments for tender mercies which have been new every morning and fresh every evening; and now, I pray thee, put forth thy hand and take thy dove into thy bosom.

—C. H. SPURGEON

JESUS, I AM RESTING, RESTING

Jesus, I am resting, resting,
In the joy of what Thou art;
I am finding out the greatness
Of Thy loving heart.
Thou hast bid me gaze upon Thee,
And Thy beauty fills my soul,
For by Thy transforming power,
Thou hast made me whole.

Jesus, I am resting, resting,
In the joy of what Thou art;
I am finding out the greatness
Of Thy loving heart.

O, how great Thy lovingkindness,
Vaster, broader than the sea!
O, how marvelous Thy goodness,
Lavished all on me!
Yes, I rest in Thee, Beloved,
Know what wealth of grace is Thine,
Know Thy certainty of promise,
And have made it mine.

Simply trusting Thee, Lord Jesus,
I behold Thee as Thou art,
And Thy love, so pure, so changeless,
Satisfies my heart;
Satisfies its deepest longings,
Meets, supplies its every need,
Compasseth me round with blessings:
Thine is love indeed!

Ever lift Thy face upon me
As I work and wait for Thee;
Resting 'neath Thy smile, Lord Jesus,
Earth's dark shadows flee.
Brightness of my Father's glory,
Sunshine of my Father's face,
Keep me ever trusting, resting,
Fill me with Thy grace.

—JEAN S. PIGOTT

BE GLAD IN THE LORD

*B*e glad in the LORD
and rejoice,
you righteous;
And shout for joy, all you
upright in heart!

—PSALM 32:11

MY QUIETNESS

*O*Thou who art my quietness, my deep repose,
My rest from strife of tongues, my holy hill,
Fair is Thy pavilion, where I hold me still.

Back let them fall from me, my clamorous foes,
Confusions multiplied;
From crowding things of sense I flee
And in Thee hide.
Until this tyranny be overpast,
Thy hand will hold me fast.

What though the tumult of the storm increase,
Grant to Thy servant strength, O Lord,
And bless with peace.

—AMY CARMICHAEL

A SONG OF ASCENTS

I lift up my eyes to the hills—where does my help
   come from?
My help comes from the LORD, the Maker of heaven
   and earth.
He will not let your foot slip—
he who watches over you will not slumber;
indeed, he who watches over Israel will neither slumber
   nor sleep.
The LORD watches over you—
the LORD is your shade at your right hand;
the sun will not harm you by day,
nor the moon by night.
The LORD will keep you from all harm—
he will watch over your life;
the LORD will watch over your coming and going
Both now and forevermore.

—PSALM 121 (NIV)

NIGHT

Thank God for night, with its great gift of sleep,
More wonderful than all His gifts to men!
For stars that walk the dreamways, and that keep
Their wide-eyed watch until dawn breaks again.
Thank God for blessed silence down the land,
More soothing than the drip of summer rain;
For darkness, soft and cool as some dear hand
Laid on a forehead feverish with pain.

Oh, only those who carry sleepless scars
Can know how sweet sleep is that comes at last;
And only the eyes that have looked long at stars
Have learned night's secret as it marches past,
Have learned to know how quiet God must keep
To guide an earth through stars that men may sleep.

—GRACE NOLL CROWELL

THE PILLAR OF THE CLOUD

Lead, Kindly Light, amid the encircling gloom,
Lead Thou me on!
The night is dark, and I am far from home—
Lead Thou me on!
Keep Thou my feet; I do not ask to see
The distant scene—one step enough for me.
I was not ever thus, nor pray'd that Thou
Shouldst lead me on.
I loved to choose and see my path; but now
Lead Thou me on!
I loved the garish day, and, spite of fears,
Pride ruled my will: remember not past years.
So long Thy power hath blest me, sure it still
Will lead me on,
O'er moor and fen, o'er crag and torrent, till
The night is gone;
And with the morn those angel faces smile
Which I have loved long since, and lost awhile.

—JOHN HENRY NEWMAN

A BURDENED AWAKENING

My thoughts had said:
Lord, I am weary of the way;
I am afraid to face another day—
Frustrated, limited,
Guarded, confined, wherever I would go
By close-set "cannots," that like hedges grow
About me now. And then our dear Lord said,
"I am about thy bed."

—AMY CARMICHAEL

ALL SHALL BE WELL

$\mathcal{B}$ut all shall be well,
  and all shall be well,
    and all manner of thing shall be well.

—JULIAN OF NORWICH

TWO THINGS HAVE I HEARD

*T*wo things have I heard:
that you, O God, are strong,
and that you, O Lord, are loving.
—PSALM 62:11–12 (NIV)

PEACE

"*P*eace I leave with you, My peace I give to you; not as the world gives do I give to you. Let not your heart be troubled, neither let it be afraid."

—JOHN 14:27

III.

As I Lay Me Down to Sleep

WE HAVE BEEN BLESSED FAR BEYOND

*W*e thank Thee with all our hearts for every gracious dispensation; for all blessings that have attended our lives; for every hour of safety, health, and peace, of domestic comfort and innocent enjoyment.

We feel that we have been blessed far beyond anything that we have deserved; and though we cannot but pray for a continuance of all these mercies, we acknowledge our unworthiness of them and implore Thee to pardon the presumption of our desires.

Keep us, O Heavenly Father, from evil this night. Bring us in safety to the beginning of another day and grant that we may rise again with every serious and religious feeling which now directs us.

May Thy mercy be extended over all mankind, bringing the ignorant to the knowledge of Thy truth, awakening the impenitent, touching the hardened. Look with compassion upon the afflicted of every condition, assuage the pangs of disease, comfort the broken in spirit.

—JANE AUSTEN

ABIDE WITH ME

Abide with me; fast falls the eventide;
The darkness deepens; Lord with me abide.
When other helpers fail and comforts flee,
Help of the helpless, O abide with me.

Not a brief glance I beg, a passing word;
But as Thou dwell'st with Thy disciples, Lord,
Familiar, condescending, patient, free.
Come not to sojourn, but abide with me.

I need Thy presence every passing hour.
What but Thy grace can foil the tempter's power?
Who, like Thyself, my guide and stay can be?
Through cloud and sunshine, Lord, abide with me.

I fear no foe, with Thee at hand to bless;

Ills have no weight, and tears no bitterness.

Where is death's sting? Where, grave, thy victory?

I triumph still, if Thou abide with me.

Hold Thou Thy cross before my closing eyes;

Shine through the gloom and point me to the skies.

Heaven's morning breaks, and earth's vain shadows
   flee;

In life, in death, O Lord, abide with me.

—HENRY F. LYTE

LORD, YOU HAVE EXAMINED ME

O LORD, You have searched me and known me. You know my sitting down and my rising up; You understand my thought afar off. You comprehend my path and my lying down, and are acquainted with all my ways. For there is not a word on my tongue, but behold, O LORD, You know it altogether. You have hedged me behind and before, and laid Your hand upon me. Such knowledge is too wonderful for me; it is high, I cannot attain it.

Where can I go from Your Spirit? Or where can I flee from Your presence? If I ascend into heaven, You are there; if I make my bed in hell, behold, You are there. If I take the wings of the morning, and dwell in the uttermost parts of the sea, even there Your hand shall lead me, and Your right hand shall hold me. If I say, "Surely the darkness shall fall on me," even the night shall be light about me; indeed, the darkness shall not hide from You, but the night shines as the day; the darkness and the light are both alike to You.

For You formed my inward parts; You covered me in my mother's womb. I will praise You, for I am fearfully and wonderfully made; marvelous are Your works, and that my soul knows very well. My frame was not hidden from You, when I was made in secret, and skillfully wrought in the lowest parts of the earth. Your eyes saw my substance, being yet unformed. And in Your book they all were written, the days fashioned for me, when as yet there were none of them.

How precious also are Your thoughts to me, O God! How great is the sum of them! If I should count them, they would be more in number than the sand; when I awake, I am still with You.

Oh, that You would slay the wicked, O God! Depart from me, therefore, you bloodthirsty men. For they speak against You wickedly; Your enemies take Your name in vain. Do I not hate them, O LORD, who hate You? And do I not loathe those who rise up against You? I hate them with perfect hatred; I count them my enemies.

Search me, O God, and know my heart; try me, and know my anxieties; and see if there is any wicked way in me, and lead me in the way everlasting.

—PSALM 139

DWELLING SAFELY

*H*e who dwells in the secret place of the Most
High shall abide under the shadow of the Almighty. I
will say of the LORD, "He is my refuge and my
fortress; my God, in Him I will trust."

Surely He shall deliver you from the snare of the
fowler and from the perilous pestilence. He shall cover
you with His feathers, and under His wings you shall
take refuge; His truth shall be your shield and buckler.
You shall not be afraid of the terror by night, nor of
the arrow that flies by day, nor of the pestilence that
walks in darkness, nor of the destruction that lays
waste at noonday.

A thousand may fall at your side, and ten thousand
at your right hand; but it shall not come near you.
Only with your eyes shall you look, and see the reward
of the wicked.

Because you have made the LORD, who is my
refuge, Even the Most High, your dwelling place, no

evil shall befall you, nor shall any plague come near your dwelling; for He shall give His angels charge over you, to keep you in all your ways. In their hands they shall bear you up, lest you dash your foot against a stone. You shall tread upon the lion and the cobra, the young lion and the serpent you shall trample underfoot.

"Because he has set his love upon Me, therefore I will deliver him; I will set him on high, because he has known My name. He shall call upon Me, and I will answer him; I will be with him in trouble; I will deliver him and honor him. With long life I will satisfy him, and show him My salvation."

—PSALM 91

NOW THE DAY IS OVER

Now the day is over,
Night is drawing nigh,
Shadows of the evening
Steal across the sky.
Now the darkness gathers,
Stars begin to peep,
Birds, and beasts and flowers
Soon will be asleep.
Jesus, give the weary
Calm and sweet repose;
With Thy tenderest blessing
May mine eyelids close.
Grant to little children
Visions bright of Thee;
Guard the sailors tossing
On the deep, blue sea.
Comfort those who suffer,
Watching late in pain;

Those who plan some evil
From their sin restrain.
Through the long night watches
May Thine angels spread
Their white wings above me,
Watching round my bed.
When the morning wakens,
Then may I arise
Pure, and fresh, and sinless
In Thy holy eyes.
Glory to the Father,
Glory to the Son,
And to Thee, blest Spirit,
While all ages run.

—SABINE BARING-GOULD

BE THOU MY VISION

*B*e Thou my Vision, O Lord of my heart;
Naught be all else to me, save that Thou art
Thou my best Thought, by day or by night,
Waking or sleeping, Thy presence my light.

—IRISH TRADITIONAL

EVENSONG

The world is still. Sunlight and moonlight meeting
   Lay long, soft shadows on the dusty road;
The sheep are folded, not a lamb is bleating.
   Fold me, O God.

The feverish hours have cooled, and ceased the
wrestling
   For place and power; hushed is the last loud word;
Only a mother calls her wayward nestling,
   "Come, little bird."

Never a stir but 'tis Thy hand that settles
   Tired flowers' affairs and piles a starry heap
Of night-lights on the jasmine. Touch my petals;
   Put me to sleep.

—AMY CARMICHAEL

THE DAY IS GENTLY
SINKING TO A CLOSE

The day is gently sinking to a close,
Fainter and yet more faint the sunlight glows:
O Brightness of Thy Father's glory,
Thou eternal Light of light, be with us now:
Where Thou art present darkness cannot be;
Midnight is glorious noon, O Lord, with Thee.
Thou, Who in darkness walking didst appear
Upon the waves, and Thy disciples cheer,
Come, Lord, in lonesome days, when storms assail,
And earthly hopes and human succors fail;
When all is dark, may we behold Thee nigh,
And hear Thy voice, "Fear not, for it is I."

—CHRISTOPHER WORDSWORTH

A PRAYER FOR PEACE

Father in Heaven! Humble before thee
   Kneeling in prayer thy children appear;
We in our weakness, we in our blindness,
   Thou in thy wisdom, hear us, oh hear!

God watching o'er us sleeps not nor slumbers,
   Faithful night watches his angels keep.
Through all the darkness, unto the dawning,
   To his beloved he giveth sleep.

—EDWARD ROWLAND SILL

THE SHADOWS OF
THE EVENING HOURS

The shadows of the evening hours fall from the
darkening sky;
Upon the fragrance of the flowers the dews of evening
lie;
Before Thy throne, O Lord of Heav'n, we kneel at
close of day;
Look on Thy children from on high, and hear us while
we pray.

The sorrows of Thy servants, Lord, O do not now
despise,
But let the incense of our prayers before Thy mercy
rise.
The brightness of the coming night upon the darkness
rolls;
With hopes of future glory, chase the shadows from
our souls.

Slowly the rays of daylight fade, so fade within our
heart
The hopes in earthly love and joy, that one by one
depart.
Slowly the bright stars, one by one, within the heavens
shine:
Give us, O Lord, fresh hopes in heaven, and trust in
things divine.

Let peace, O Lord, Thy peace, O God, upon our souls
descend;
From midnight fears and perils, now our trembling
hearts defend.
Give us a respite from our toil; calm and subdue our
woes.
Through the long day we labor, Lord, O give us now
repose.

—ADELAIDE ANNE PROCTER

QUIETNESS

$\mathcal{D}$rop thy still dews of quietness till all our
striving cease;
Take from our souls the strain and stress,
And let our ordered lives confess
The beauty of thy peace.
—JOHN GREENLEAF WHITTIER

EVENING PRAYER

My Heavenly Father, I thank You, through Jesus Christ, Your beloved Son, that You have protected me, by Your grace. Forgive, I pray, all my sins and the evil I have done. Protect me, by Your grace, tonight. I put myself in Your care, body and soul and all that I have. Let Your holy angels be with me, so that the evil enemy will not gain power over me. Amen.

—MARTIN LUTHER

ON GOING TO BED

As my head rests on my pillow,
Let my soul rest in your mercy.

As my limbs relax on my mattress,
Let my soul relax in your peace.

As my body finds warmth beneath the blankets,
Let my soul find warmth in your love.

As my mind is filled with dreams,
Let my soul be filled with visions of heaven.

—JOHANN FREYLINGHAUSEN

COME TO ME

Come to Me, all you who labor and are heavy laden, and I will give you rest. Take My yoke upon you and learn from Me, for I am gentle and lowly in heart, and you will find rest for your souls. For My yoke is easy and My burden is light.

—MATTHEW 11:28–30

SLEEP

Thou hast promised thy beloved sleep;
Give me restoring rest needful for tomorrow's toil;
If dreams be mine, let them not be tinged with evil.
Let thy Spirit make my time of repose
    a blessed temple of his holy presence.

May my frequent lying down make me familiar with death,
the bed I approach remind me of the grave,
the eyes I now close picture to me their final closing.
Keep me always ready, waiting for admittance to thy presence.
Weaken my attachment to earthly things.
May I hold life loosely in my hand,
    Knowing that I receive it on condition of its surrender;
As pain and suffering betoken transitory health,
    may I not shrink from a death that introduces me
    to the freshness of eternal youth.
I retire this night in full assurance of one day awaking with
thee.
All glory for this precious hope,
    for the gospel of grace,
    for thine unspeakable gift of Jesus,
    for the fellowship of the Trinity.

Withhold not thy mercies in the night season;
    thy hand never wearies,
    thy power needs no repose,
    thine eye never sleeps.

Help me when I helpless lie,
    when my conscience accuses me of sin,
    when my mind is harassed by foreboding thoughts,
    when my eyes are held awake by personal anxieties.

Show thyself to me as the God of all grace, love, and
power;
    thou hast a balm for every wound,
    a solace for all anguish,
    a remedy for every pain,
    a peace for all disquietude.
Permit me to commit myself to thee awake or asleep.

                     —THE VALLEY OF VISION

ROCKED IN THE CRADLE
OF THE DEEP

Rocked in the cradle of the deep
I lay me down in peace to sleep;
Secure I rest upon the wave,
For Thou, O Lord! hast power to save.
I know Thou wilt not slight my call,
For Thou dost mark the sparrow's fall;
And calm and peaceful shall I sleep,
Rocked in the cradle of the deep.

When in the dead of night I lie
And gaze upon the trackless sky,
The star-bespangled heavenly scroll,
The boundless waters as they roll,
I feel Thy wondrous power to save
From perils of the stormy wave:
Rocked in the cradle of the deep,
I calmly rest and soundly sleep.

And such the trust that still were mine,
Though stormy winds swept o'er the brine,
Or though the tempest's fiery breath
Roused me from sleep to wreck and death.
In ocean cave, still safe with Thee
The germ of immortality!
And calm and peaceful shall I sleep,
Rocked in the cradle of the deep.

—EMMA HART WILLARD

Prayers

PRAYER IN THE NIGHT

I'm wide awake, Lord, unable to turn my mind off. I keep going over and over the events of the day. I worry about what I said and did, reconstructing conversations and encounters in a thousand different ways. I wish I could turn my mind off. I need sleep, but it's like the accelerator of my mind is racing, racing, racing.

God, why don't you help me sleep?!

I guess at a time like this I'm supposed to feel pious and pray. But I don't want to pray; I want to sleep. Why can't I turn my mind off? I'm so tired.

God, can't you simply induce sleep—the great cosmic tranquilizer? I guess I wouldn't want that even if it were possible. But I do want sleep.

God why can't I sleep? Why can't I sleep?

Shalom, my child, shalom. You are anxious for many things. Rest. Rest. Rest in my love. Sleep is not necessary if you rest in my love.

—RICHARD FOSTER

INSOMNIA

    E'en this, Lord, didst thou bless—
This pain of sleeplessness—
    The livelong night,
Urging God's gentlest angel from thy side,
That anguish only might with thee abide
    Until the light.
Yea, e'en the last and best,
Thy victory and rest,
    Came thus to thee;
For 'twas while others calmly slept around,
That thou alone in sleeplessness wast found
    To comfort me.

              —JOHN BANISTER TABB

THE NIGHT ALSO IS THINE

*Y*es, Lord, thou dost not abdicate thy throne when the sun goeth down, nor dost thou leave the world; . . . thine eyes watch us as the stars, and thine arms surround us as the zodiac belts the sky. The dews of kindly sleep and all the influences of the moon are in thy hand, and the alarms and solemnities of night are equally with thee. This is very sweet to me when watching through the midnight hours, or tossing to and fro in anguish. There are precious fruits put forth by the moon as well as by the sun: may my Lord make me to be a favoured partaker in them.

—C. H. SPURGEON

UNDER HIS WINGS

Under His wings I am safely abiding,
Though the night deepens and tempests are wild,
Still I can trust Him; I know He will keep me,
He has redeemed me, and I am His child.

Under His wings, under His wings,
Who from His love can sever?
Under His wings my soul shall abide,
Safely abide forever.

Under His wings, what a refuge in sorrow!
How the heart yearningly turns to His rest!
Often when earth has no balm for my healing,
There I find comfort, and there I am blessed.

Under His wings, oh, what precious enjoyment!
There will I hide till life's trials are o'er;
Sheltered, protected, no evil can harm me,
Resting in Jesus, I'm safe evermore.

—WILLIAM O. CUSHING

CREATOR OF THE EARTH AND SKY

Creator of the earth and sky,
Ruling the firmament on high,
Clothing the day with robes of light,
Blessing with gracious sleep the night.
That rest may comfort weary men,
And brace to useful toil again,
And soothe awhile the harassed mind,
And sorrow's heavy load unbind.
Day sinks; we thank Thee for Thy gift;
Night comes; and once again we lift
Our prayer and vows and hymns that we
Against all ills may shielded be.
That when black darkness closes day,
And shadows thicken round our way,
Faith may no darkness know, and night
From faith's clear beam may borrow light.
Rest not, my heaven born mind and will;
Rest, all the thoughts and deeds of ill;

May faith its watch unwearied keep,
And cool the dreaming warmth of sleep.
From cheats of sense, Lord, keep me free;
And let my heart's depth dream of Thee;
Let not my envious foe draw near,
To break my rest with any fear.
Pray we the Father and the Son,
And Holy Ghost: O Three in One,
Blest Trinity, Whom all obey,
Guard Thou Thy sheep by night and day.

—AMBROSE OF MILAN

YOU ALONE

I will both lie down in peace,
And sleep;
For You alone, O LORD,
Make me dwell in safety.

—PSALM 4:8

PRECIOUS LORD, TAKE MY HAND

Precious Lord, take my hand.

Lead me on. Let me stand.

I am tired. I am weak. I am worn.

Through the storm,

Through the night,

Lead me on to the light.

Take my hand, precious Lord,

And lead me home.

—AFRICAN AMERICAN SPIRITUAL

THE DAY IS PAST AND GONE

Lord, keep us safe this night,
Secure from all our fears;
May angels guard us while we sleep,
Till morning light appears.

—JOHN LELAND

I REMEMBER YOU

*W*hen I remember You on my bed,
I meditate on You in the night watches.
Because You have been my help,
Therefore in the shadow of Your wings I will rejoice.
My soul follows close behind You;
Your right hand upholds me.

—PSALM 63:6–8

GOOD NIGHT!

Good night, dear Lord! And now
Let them that loved to keep
Thy little bed in Bethlehem,
Be near me while I sleep;
For I—more helpless, Lord—of them
Have greater need than Thou.

—JOHN BANISTER TABB

IV.

Bedtime Prayers for Others

PRAYER

Gather up
In the arms of your pity
The sick, the depraved,
The desperate, the tired,
All the scum
Of our weary city
Gather up
In the arms of your pity
Gather up
In the arms of your love—
Those who expect
No love from above.

—LANGSTON HUGHES

FOR A YOUNG CHILD'S FUTURE

*L*ord, as I stand beside this crib,
watching this little boy fall asleep . . .
his blond curls sticking to his small, damp forehead,
his chubby fingers wrapped tightly around his blanket,
my heart is filled with emotion, wonder, and awe.
I have so many dreams and ambitions for him.

Please help me to remember that he is first of all Yours,
and that the most important thing of all is that he grow to
love You and follow You. So, Lord, tonight I put aside any
and all prayers that could have roots in selfish motherly
desires, and pray these words for him,

Beloved child, be steadfast, immovable, always abounding
in the work of the Lord. (1 Cor. 15:58)

Because, Lord, if this prayer is answered, then one day I
will be able to say with John that my greatest joy is know-
ing that my children are walking in the truth.

—GIGI GRAHAM TCHIVIDJIAN

AN EVENING PRAYER FOR OTHERS

*W*atch, Lord,

With those who wake, or watch, or weep tonight,

And give your angels charge over those who sleep.

Tend your sick ones, O Lord Jesus Christ,

Rest your weary ones; bless your dying ones;

Soothe your suffering ones; pity your afflicted ones;

Shield your joyous ones.

All for your love's sake.

—SAINT AUGUSTINE

FOR ALL WHO NEED

For all who watch tonight—by land or sea or air—
O Father, may they know that Thou art with them
there.

For all who weep tonight, the hearts that cannot rest,
Reveal Thy love, that wondrous love which gave for us
Thy best.

For all who wake tonight, love's tender watch to keep,
Watcher Divine, Thyself draw nigh, Thou who dost
never sleep.

For all who fear tonight, whate'er the dread may be,
We ask for them the perfect peace of hearts that rest
in Thee.

Our own beloved tonight, O Father, keep, and where
Our love and succor cannot reach, now bless them
through our prayer.

And all who pray tonight, Thy wrestling hosts, O
Lord,
Make weakness strong, let them prevail according to
Thy word.

—AUTHOR UNKNOWN

GOD KEEP YOU

God keep you, dearest, all this lonely night:
   The winds are still,
   The moon drops down behind the western hill;
God keep you safely, dearest, till the light.

God keep you then when slumber melts away,
   And care and strife
   Take up new arms to fret our waking life,
God keep you through the battle of the day.

God keep you. Nay, beloved soul, how vain,
   How poor is prayer!
I can but say again, and yet again,
   God keep you every time and everywhere.

—MADELINE BRIDGES

A Prayer for New Believers

"For [your sake] I kneel before the Father, from whom his whole family in heaven and on earth derives its name. I pray that out of his glorious riches he may strengthen you with power through his Spirit in your inner being, so that Christ may dwell in your hearts through faith. And I pray that you, being rooted and established in love, may have power, together with all the saints, to grasp how wide and long and high and deep is the love of Christ, and to know this love that surpasses knowledge—that you may be filled to the measure of all the fullness of God."

—EPHESIANS 3:14-19 (NIV)

A PRAYER FOR THE SICK

At even, ere the sun was set,
The sick, O Lord, around Thee lay;
O, with how many pains they met!
O, with what joy they went away!
Once more 'tis eventide, and we,
Oppressed with various ills, draw near;
What if Thyself we cannot see?
We know that Thou art ever near.
O Savior Christ, our woes dispel;
For some are sick, and some are sad;
And some have never loved Thee well,
And some have lost the love they had.
And some are pressed with worldly care
And some are tried with sinful doubt;
And some such grievous passions tear,
That only Thou canst cast them out.
And none, O Lord, have perfect rest,
For none are wholly free from sin;

And they who fain would serve Thee best

Are conscious most of wrong within.

O Savior Christ, Thou too art man;

Thou has been troubled, tempted, tried;

Thy kind but searching glance can scan

The very wounds that shame would hide.

Thy touch has still its ancient power.

No word from Thee can fruitless fall;

Hear, in this solemn evening hour,

And in Thy mercy heal us all.

—HENRY TWELLS

FOR THE RULERS OF THE NATIONS

Today, O God, I hold before you the rulers of the nations—Kings, Queens, Presidents, Prime Ministers—all who are in positions of supreme leadership.

I can be quick to criticize: help me, Lord, to first enter their dilemma. On most issues of state I have the luxury of withholding judgment, of not committing myself, of sitting on the fence. Even when I have an opinion, it has little influence and seldom any consequence. Not so with the rulers of the nations. To the extent that they really lead, they must make decisions, even if they are poor ones.

Help these leaders, O God, in the loneliness of their decisions. Put wise counselors around them.

Take, I pray, the bits and pieces of virtue that are in each ruler and cause them to grow and mature. And take all the destructive motives and cause them to vanish like smoke in the wind.

Lord, I know that many—perhaps most—rulers do

not know you, nor do they seek you. But you seek them! Help them see how good right decisions are. And where decisions must be made that are not in their own interest, deepen their sense of duty. Having seen the light, give them the courage to walk in the light.

Amen.

—RICHARD FOSTER

A Prayer for Spiritual Leaders

I pray, dear God, for our spiritual leaders.
Increase in them the charism of *faith* that they might
preach the Word of God with boldness.
Increase in them the charism of *wisdom* that they might
guide us into the Way.
Increase in them the charism of *pastor* that they might
always lead us with compassion and strength.
I intercede, O Lord, for our spiritual leaders.
Grow in them the fruit of *gentleness* that they might under-
stand our frailty.
Grow in them the fruit of *peace* that they might be free of
manipulation.
Grow in them the fruit of *love* that they might always serve
out of a divine wellspring.
I plead, gracious Father, for our spiritual leaders.
Protect them from the *attacks* of the evil one.
Protect them from the *distractions* that render their work
ineffective.
Protect them from the *criticism* of well-meaning people.
All these things I ask in the name of Jesus Christ.
Amen.

—Richard Foster

A PRAYER FOR MISSIONARIES

Eternal Father, who art loving unto every man, and hast given thy Son to be the Saviour of the world: Grant that the pure light of his Gospel may overcome the darkness of idolatry in every land and that all the lost children, dwelling in far countries, may be brought home to thee. Protect the messengers of the Gospel amid all perils; guide them through all perplexities; give them wisdom, strength, and courage, to make known by word and life the grace of our Lord Jesus; prosper all that they do in his blessed name, to serve the bodies and the souls of men; hasten, we beseech thee, the promised day, when at the name of Jesus every knee shall bow and every tongue confess that he is Lord; to the glory of God the Father. Amen.

—HENRY VAN DYKE

V.

Bedtime Prayers for Holidays and Memorable Days

A FAMILY PRAYER

O God, make the door of this house wide enough to receive all who need human love and fellowship; narrow enough to shut out all envy, pride, and strife. Make its threshold smooth enough to be no stumbling block to children, nor to straying feet, but rugged and strong enough to turn back the tempter's power. God, make the door of this house the gateway to thine eternal kingdom.

—BISHOP THOMAS KEN

EASTER PRAYER

It is only right, with all the powers of our heart and mind, to praise You Father and Your only-begotten Son, our Lord Jesus Christ. Dear Father, by Your wondrous condescension of lovingkindness toward us, Your servants, You gave up Your Son. Dear Jesus, You paid the debt of Adam for us to the Eternal Father by Your blood poured forth in lovingkindness. You cleared away the darkness of sin by Your magnificent and radiant resurrection. You broke the bonds of death and rose from the grave as a Conqueror. You reconciled Heaven and earth. Our life had no hope of eternal happiness before You redeemed us. Your resurrection has washed away our sins, restored our innocence, and brought us joy. How inestimable is the tenderness of Your love!

We pray You, Lord, to preserve Your servants in the peaceful enjoyment of this Easter happiness. We ask this through Jesus Christ Our Lord, who lives and reigns with God the Father, in the unity of the Holy Spirit, forever and ever. Amen.

—SAINT GREGORY

TODAY IS MY BIRTHDAY

*O*Loving God, today is my birthday.

For your care from the day I was born until today

And for your love, I thank you.

Help me to be strong and healthy,

And to show love for others, as Jesus did.

—AUTHOR UNKNOWN

A BLESSING ON MOTHER'S DAY

Mother in gladness, Mother in sorrow

Mother today, and Mother tomorrow,

With arms ever open to fold and caress you,

O Mother of Mine, may God keep you and bless you.

—W. DAYTON WEDGEFARTH

A Father's Day Prayer

Thank you, friend Jesus,
for my father who loves me,
for my grandfather who cares for me,
and for God, your father and mine,
who made me and is always with me.
How lucky I am!

— GAYNELL BORDES CRONIN

A MEMORIAL DAY PRAYER

*L*ord God of Hosts, in whom our fathers trusted: We give thee thanks for all thy servants who have laid down their lives in the service of our country. Unite all the people of this nation in a holy purpose to defend the freedom and brotherhood for which they lived and died. Grant, we beseech thee, that the liberty they bequeathed unto us may be continued to our children and our children's children, and that the power of the Gospel may here abound, to the blessing of all the nations of the earth, and to thine eternal glory; through Jesus Christ thy Son our Lord. Amen.

—HENRY VAN DYKE

AFTER THE DEATH
OF A LOVED ONE

*L*ord, another lamb will join the fold tonight.
Good Shepherd, welcome her, we pray, and hold her
tight.

—RUTH BELL GRAHAM

MAKE ME AN INSTRUMENT OF THY PEACE

*L*ord, make me an instrument of your peace.

Where there is hatred, let me sow love;

where there is injury, pardon;

where there is doubt, faith;

where there is despair, hope;

where there is darkness, light;

and where there is sadness, joy.

Divine Master, grant that I may not so much seek to

be consoled as to console;

to be understood as to understand;

to be loved as to love.

For it is in giving that we receive;

it is in pardoning that we are pardoned;

and it is in dying that we are born to eternal life.

—SAINT FRANCIS OF ASSISI

A Prayer for Our Country

O eternal God, through whose mighty power our fathers won their liberties of old: Grant, we beseech thee, that we and all the people of this land may have grace to maintain these liberties in righteousness and peace, through Jesus Christ our Lord. Amen.

—Author Unknown

A PRAYER OF THANKSGIVING

*L*ord, behold our family here assembled.
We thank Thee
 For this place in which we dwell;
For the peace accorded us this day,
For the hope with which we expect tomorrow;
For the health, the work, the food
And the bright skies that make our lives delightful,
For our friends in all parts of the earth, and our
friendly helpers . . .
Let peace abound in our small company.

—ROBERT LOUIS STEVENSON

WE THANK THEE

For flowers that bloom about our feet,
For tender grass so fresh, so sweet,
For the song of bird and hum of bee,
For all things fair we hear or see,
Father in heaven, we thank Thee!

For blue of stream and blue of sky,
For pleasant shade of branches high,
For fragrant air and cooling breeze,
For beauty of the blooming trees,
Father in heaven, we thank Thee.

For each new morning with its light,
For rest and shelter of the night,
For health and food, for love and friends,
For everything Thy goodness sends,
Father in heaven, we thank Thee.

—RALPH WALDO EMERSON

A CHRISTMAS EVE PRAYER

O God our Loving father, help us rightly to remember the birth of Jesus that we may share in the song of the angels, the gladness of the shepherds, and the worship of the wise men.

Close the door of hate, and open the door of love all over the world.

Deliver us from evil by the blessing that Christ brings, and teach us to be merry with clear hearts.

May the Christmas morning make us happy to be Thy children and the Christmas evening bring us to our beds with grateful thoughts, forgiving and forgiven, for Jesus' sake. Amen.

— ROBERT LOUIS STEVENSON

A CHRISTMAS PRAYER

O holy Child of Bethlehem!
Descend to us, we pray;
Cast out our sin, and enter in,
Be born in us today!
—PHILLIPS BROOKS

THE DAY AFTER CHRISTMAS

O Lord Jesus, we thank Thee for the joys of this season, for the divine love that was shed abroad among men when Thou didst first come as a little child.

But may we not think of Thy coming as a distant event that took place once and has never been repeated. May we know that Thou art still here walking among us, by our sides, whispering over our shoulders, tugging at our sleeves, smiling upon us when we need encouragement and help.

We thank Thee for Thy spirit that moves at this season the hearts of men: to be kindly and thoughtful—where before they were careless and indifferent; to be generous—where before they lived in selfishness; to be gentle—where before they had been rough and unmindful of the weak; to express their love—where before it had been taken for granted and assumed.

We are learning—O Lord, so slowly—life's true values. Surely Christmas would teach us the unforgettable lesson of the things that matter most—the ties that bind the structure of the family upon which our country and all the world rests; the love that we have for one another which binds Thy whole creation to Thy footstool, Thy throne. We are learning slowly, but, O God, we thank Thee that we are learning.

So may Christmas linger with us, even as Thou art beside us the whole year through. Amen.

—PETER MARSHALL

A Prayer for a New Home

*D*ear Lord, we've prayed
and planned
and built this house,
and here we pause,
for You alone
can by Your presence hallow it
and make this house a home.

—Ruth Bell Graham

A BED IN MY HEART

Ah, dearest Jesus, holy Child,
Make Thee a bed, soft, undefiled,
Within my heart, that it may be
A quiet chamber kept for Thee.
My heart for very joy doth leap,
My lips no more can silence keep.
I too must sing, with joyful tongue,
That sweetest ancient cradle song,
Glory to God in highest heaven,
Who unto man His Son hath given,
While angels sing with pious mirth,
A glad New Year to all the earth.

—MARTIN LUTHER

ANOTHER YEAR IS DAWNING

Another year is dawning, dear Father, let it be
In working or in waiting, another year with Thee.
Another year of progress, another year of praise,
Another year of proving Thy presence all the days.
Another year of mercies, of faithfulness and grace,
Another year of gladness in the shining of Thy face;
Another year of leaning upon Thy loving breast;
Another year of trusting, of quiet, happy rest.
Another year of service, of witness for Thy love,
Another year of training for holier work above.
Another year is dawning, dear Father, let it be
On earth, or else in heaven, another year for Thee.

—FRANCES RIDLEY HAVERGAL

VI.

Bedtime Prayers
for Children

FATHER, WE THANK THEE FOR THE NIGHT

Father, we thank Thee for the night,
And for the pleasant morning light;
For rest and food and loving care,
And all that makes the world so fair.

Help us to do the things we should,
To be to others kind and good;
In all we do, in work or play,
To love Thee better day by day.

—REBECCA WESTON

GOD IS WITH ME

The day is past, the sun is set,
And the white stars are in the sky;
While the long grass with dew is wet,
And through the air the bats now fly.

The lambs have now lain down to sleep,
The birds have long since sought their nests;
The air is still; and dark, and deep
On the hillside the old wood rests.

Yet of the dark I have no fear,
But feel as safe as when 'tis light;
For I know God is with me there,
And he will guard me through the night.

For God is by me when I pray,
And when I close my eyes in sleep,
I know that he will with me stay,
And will all night watch by me keep.

For he who rules the stars and sea,
Who makes the grass and trees to grow,
Will look on a poor child like me,
When on my knees to him I bow.

He holds all things in his right hand,
The rich, the poor, the great, the small;
When we sleep, or sit, or stand,
Is with us, for he loves us all.

—THOMAS MILLER

LOVING FATHER, PUT AWAY

*L*oving Father, put away
All the wrong I've done today;
Make me sorry, true, and good;
Make me love thee as I should;
Make me feel by day and night
I am ever in thy sight.

Heavenly Father, hear my prayer,
Take thy child into thy care;
Let thy angels pure and bright
Watch around me through the night. Amen.
—AUTHOR UNKNOWN

WORDS OF LIGHT

Fear thou not the cloudy evening.
By dim waters fireflies glisten;
'Mid the dark leaves of the tree
Starry hosts are moving; listen,
Listen for they speak to thee:
"My Lord will take care of me."

Fear thou not the moonless darkness.
Moonless nights discover fireflies,
Star-seeds of eternity,
Luminous when common day dies.
Words of light are sown for thee:
"My Lord will take care of me."

—AMY CARMICHAEL

CAN YOU COUNT THE STARS?

Can you count the stars that brightly
Twinkle in the midnight sky?
Can you count the clouds, so lightly
O'er the meadows floating by?
God, the Lord, doth mark their number,
With His eyes that never slumber;
He hath made them every one,
He hath made them every one.

—JOHANN W. HEY

THE LORD IS MY SHEPHERD

The LORD is my shepherd; I shall not want.

He makes me to lie down in green pastures; He leads
me beside the still waters.

He restores my soul; He leads me in the paths of
righteousness for His name's sake.

Yea, though I walk through the valley of the shadow
of death, I will fear no evil; for You are with me;
Your rod and Your staff, they comfort me.

You prepare a table before me in the presence of my
enemies; You anoint my head with oil; my cup runs
over.

Surely goodness and mercy shall follow me all the days
of my life; and I will dwell in the house of the LORD
forever.

—PSALM 23

LORD, KEEP US SAFE THIS NIGHT

*L*ord, keep us safe this night.
Secure from all our fears.
May angels guard us while we sleep,
Till morning light appears.

—AUTHOR UNKNOWN

FROM GHOULIES AND GHOSTIES

From ghoulies and ghosties and long-
leggity beasties,
and all things that go bump in the night,
Good Lord, deliver us.
—TRADITIONAL SCOTTISH

A PRAYER FOR THE ANIMALS

O heavenly Father,

protect and bless all things that have breath:

guard them from evil and let them sleep in peace.

—ALBERT SCHWEITZER

GOD IS NEAR

I hear no voice, I feel no touch,
    I see no glory bright;
But yet I know that God is near,
    In darkness as in light.

He watches ever by my side,
    And hears my whispered prayer:
The Father for His little child
    Both night and day doth care.

—AUTHOR UNKNOWN

MY FATHER, HEAR MY PRAYER

My Father, hear my prayer
Before I go to rest;
It is Thy trustful child
That cometh to be blest.
Forgive me all my sin,
And let me sleep this night
In safety and in peace
Until the morning light.
Lord, help me every day
To love Thee more and more,
And try to do Thy will
Much better than before.
Now look upon me, Lord,
Ere I lie down to rest;
It is Thy trustful child
That cometh to be blest.

—AUTHOR UNKNOWN

GOD BLESS ALL

God bless all those that I love,
God bless all those that love me.
God bless all those that love those that I love,
and those that love those who love me.

—AMERICAN TRADITIONAL

JESUS, TENDER SHEPHERD

Jesus, tender Shepherd, hear me
Bless thy little lamb tonight;
Through the darkness be Thou near me,
Keep me safe till morning light.
All this day Thy hand has led me,
And I thank Thee for Thy care;
Thou has warmed me, clothed and fed me;
Listen to my evening prayer.

Let my sins all be forgiven;
Bless the friends I love so well:
Take us all at last to heaven,
Happy there with Thee to dwell.

—MARY DUNCAN

LORD, WHEN WE HAVE NOT ANY LIGHT

Lord, when we have not any light,
And mothers are asleep;
Then through the stillness of the night,
Thy little children keep.
When shadows haunt the quiet room,
Help us to understand
That Thou art with us through the gloom,
To hold us by the hand.
And though we do not always see
The holy angels near,
O may we trust ourselves to Thee,
Nor have one foolish fear.
So in the morning may we wake,
When wakes the kindly sun,
More loving for our Father's sake
To each unloving one.

—ANNIE MATHESON

NOW I LAY ME DOWN TO SLEEP

Now I lay me down to sleep,
I pray Thee, Lord, Thy child to keep;
Thy love go with me all the night,
And wake me with the morning light.

—AUTHOR UNKNOWN

GOOD NIGHT PRAYER

Father, unto Thee I pray,
Thou hast guarded me all day;
Safe I am while in Thy sight,
Safely let me sleep tonight.

Bless my friends, the whole world bless;
Help me to learn helpfulness;
Keep me ever in Thy sight;
So to all I say goodnight.

—HENRY JOHNSTONE

GOOD NIGHT

Good Night! Good Night!
Far flies the light;
But still God's love
Shall flame above,
Making all bright.
Good night! Good night!
—VICTOR HUGO

SLEEP, BABY, SLEEP

Sleep, baby, sleep!
Thy father guards the sheep,
Thy mother shakes the dreamland tree,
And from it fall sweet dreams for thee;
Sleep, baby, sleep!
Sleep, baby, sleep!

Sleep, baby, sleep!
The large stars are the sheep,
The little ones the lambs, I guess,
The gentle moon the shepherdess,
Sleep, baby, sleep!
Sleep, baby, sleep!

Sleep, baby, sleep!
Our Savior loves His sheep,
He is the Lamb of God on high,
Who for our sakes came down to die,
Sleep, baby, sleep!
Sleep, baby, sleep!

—GERMAN TRADITIONAL

SLEEP

Sleep, little baby of mine;
Dear little heart be at rest,
For Jesus, like you,
Was a baby once too,
And slept on His own mother's breast.

Shut little sleepy blue eyes,
Night and darkness are near—
But Jesus looks down
Through the shadows that frown,
And baby has nothing to fear.

Sleep, little baby of mine,
Soft on your pillow so white;
Jesus is here
To watch over you, dear,
And nothing can harm you tonight.

Oh, little darling of mine,

What can you know of the bliss,

The comfort I keep,

Awake and asleep,

Because I am certain of this.

—AUTHOR UNKNOWN

A CRADLE HYMN

Hush! my dear, lie still and slumber,
Holy angels guard thy bed!
Heavenly blessings without number
Gently falling on thy head.

Sleep, my babe; thy food and raiment,
House and home, thy friends provide;
All without thy care or payment:
All thy wants are well supplied.

How much better thou'rt attended
Than the Son of God could be,
When from heaven He descended
And became a child like thee!

Soft and easy is thy cradle:
Coarse and hard thy Saviour lay,
When His birthplace was a stable
And His softest bed was hay.

Blessed babe! what glorious features—
Spotless fair, divinely bright!

Must He dwell with brutal creatures

How could angels bear the sight?

Was there nothing but a manger

Cursed sinners could afford

To receive the heavenly stranger?

Did they thus affront their Lord?

Soft, my child: I did not chide thee,

Though my song might sound too hard;

'Tis thy mother sits beside thee,

And her arms shall be thy guard.

Yet to read the shameful story

How the Jews abused their King,

How they served the Lord of Glory,

Makes me angry while I sing.

See the kinder shepherds round Him,

Telling wonders from the sky!

Where they sought Him, there they found Him,

With His virgin mother by.

See the lovely babe a-dressing;

Lovely infant, how He smiled!

When He wept, the mother's blessing

Soothed and hush'd the holy child.

Lo, He slumbers in His manger,
Where the horned oxen fed:
Peace, my darling: here's no danger,
Here's no ox anear thy bed.
'Twas to save thee, child, from dying,
Save my dear from burning flame,
Bitter groans and endless crying,
That thy blest Redeemer came.
May'st thou live to know and fear Him,
Trust and love Him all thy days:
Then go dwell for ever near Him,
See His face, and sing His praise!

—Isaac Watts

ALL THROUGH THE NIGHT

Sleep my love, and peace attend thee
All through the night;
Guardian angels God will lend thee,
All through the night,
Soft the drowsy hours are creeping,
Hill and vale in slumber steeping,
I my loving vigil keeping,
All through the night.
Angels watching ever round thee,
All through the night,
In thy slumbers close surround thee,
All through the night,
They should of all fears disarm thee,
No forebodings should alarm thee,
They will let no peril harm thee,
All through the night.

—AUTHOR UNKNOWN

BE NEAR ME, LORD JESUS

Be near me, Lord Jesus, I ask Thee to stay,

Close by me forever, and love me, I pray.

Bless all the dear children in Thy tender care,

And take us to heaven to live with Thee there.

—MARTIN LUTHER

VII.

Our Family's Own Special Prayers

Bedtime

Prayers

Our Family's Special Prayers

Acknowledgments

$\mathscr{G}$rateful acknowledgment is made to the following publishers for use of material from their previously published works. Every effort has been made to locate the original sources of these prayers. However, in many cases the sources may no longer be available, or the prayer may be attributed to many different sources. Inadvertent omissions, if called to the publisher's attention, will be noted in future editions.

Amy Carmichael: from *Mountain Breezes,* © 1999 The Dohnavur Fellowship, Fort Washington, PA.

Gaynell Bordes Cronin, "A Father's Day Prayer" from *Friend Jesus: Prayers for Children,* St. Anthony Messenger Press, Cincinnati, OH.

Grace Noll Crowell: all poems from *Songs for Courage,* © 1938, Harper Collins, NY.

Richard Foster: all prayers from *Prayers from the Heart,* © 1994, Harper Collins, NY.

Ruth Bell Graham, Gigi Graham Tchividjian: from *Prayers for a Mother's Day,* © 1999, Nelson Books. Reprinted by permission of Thomas Nelson Inc., Nashville, TN.

Langston Hughes: from *The Collected Poems of Langston Hughes,* ed. Arnold Rampersad, © 1994, Alfred A. Knopf (a division of Random House).

Acknoledgments

John Kirvan: from *Grace Through Simplicity,* © 2004 by Quest Associates. Permission granted by Ave Maria Press, P.O. Box 428, Notre Dame, IN 46556.

Catherine Marshall: from *Adventures in Prayer,* Chosen Books, Grand Rapids, MI.

Peter Marshall: from *The Prayers of Peter Marshall,* © 1949, 1950, 1951, 1954, 1982, Chosen Books (a division of Baker Publishing Group), Grand Rapids, MI.

TABLE GRACES
for the
FAMILY

Mealtime presents a wonderful opportunity not only to reconnect with the family—catch up on the day's events, soccer scores and personal victories—but also to reconnect with God, thanking him for the glory of the day and those personal victories. With more than one hundred readings, compiled from Scripture, poets and well-known church leaders, *Table Graces for the Family*, ensures a variety of choices for a variety of days. Besides special prayers for family occasions, religious and national holidays, a selection of musical blessings rounds out a collection that promises to nourish the soul.

W PUBLISHING GROUP
A Division of Thomas Nelson Publishers
Since 1798

www.wpublishinggroup.com